Portuguese Macau: The History and Legacy of the Autonomous Territory that Became the Last European Colony in Asia

By Charles River Editors

A picture of Macau around 1870

About Charles River Editors

CHARLES RIVER
E D I T O R S

Charles River Editors is a boutique digital publishing company, specializing in bringing history back to life with educational and engaging books on a wide range of topics. Keep up to date with our new and free offerings with this 5 second sign up on our weekly mailing list, and visit Our Kindle Author Page to see other recently published Kindle titles.

We make these books for you and always want to know our readers' opinions, so we encourage you to leave reviews and look forward to publishing new and exciting titles each week.

Introduction

A picture of the "O Porto Interior" in Macau around 1900

Portuguese Macau

During the 15th century, China had become economically and technologically advanced compared to civilizations in Europe at the time, and its fleet, which had reached a total of 3,500 ships, was unmatched by any other world power. Nevertheless, after conducting several trade expeditions with the massive fleet, the Chinese ships were either burned in the docks or left to rot. With that, China began to revert to the xenophobic policies of its past and reduce its presence in other lands. By 1525, the largest naval fleet in the world had essentially been destroyed or dismantled by China itself.

While China was in the process of isolating itself from the rest of the world, the European explorers were beginning to discover new lands, such as North America and South America. Among the countries doing the most exploring during this time were the Portuguese. The Portuguese had reached India in 1498, and by 1509 they had established part of their empire in India. This allowed the Portuguese to have a base of operations to further expand east into Asia. In 1511, the Portuguese captured the large spice trading center of Malacca in Malaysia, and like their base in India, Malacca allowed the Portuguese to have a foothold, thereby providing access to China and Southeast Asia (Brinkley 1904).

The Portuguese explorer Jorge Álvares visited the Chinese coast in 1513 and was the first European to do so via the sea. Shortly after, more Portuguese visited around the Tunmen Inlet, which is believed to have been somewhere around the Pearl River Delta, and an establishment was set up there in 1514. At this time the Chinese knew nothing of the Portuguese other than their violent takeover of Malacca, a tributary to the Chinese Empire, so the Portuguese were treated with caution.

In 1516, Rafael Perestrello was dispatched from Malacca to the islands of Guangdong where his people were well received. Due to this favorable reception, more ships and trading vessels were sent the following year under the command of Perez de Andrade. The fleet anchored on the island Shang-chuan and was at first viewed with suspicion, given the frequent raids from Japanese pirates around the Guangdong region. However, Andrade was peaceful in his dealings with the Chinese and the Chinese allowed two of his ships to proceed to Guangzhou (Canton), while the others returned to Malacca or sailed up the coast with Chinese junks to other merchant factories. The peaceful interactions with the Portuguese was not to last for very long thanks to Andrade's brother, Simão de Andrade, also known as Simon (Brinkley 1904: 170-142).

The Portuguese fleet that arrived in 1518 under the command of Andrade's brother quickly turned to piracy, and the diplomatic relations between the Chinese and Portuguese deteriorated. At the time, an envoy was in Beijing, where they had been peacefully welcomed, but after hearing news of the actions of Portuguese (led by Simão de Andrade), the Chinese demanded of the visiting envoy that the Portuguese leave Malacca (since it was a tributary of China). The envoy refused and was thrown in prison, where one of the Portuguese diplomats was executed. The rest of the envoy was eventually shipped off to prison in Guangzhou.

The hostile activities of the Portuguese are mainly attributed to Simão de Andrade, who was accused of kidnapping Chinese boys and girls for prostitution, although he is also said to have attempted establishing a fort on one of the islands. The establishment of a fort would have been viewed as a hostile invasion on the part of the Portuguese, much the same way Malacca was invaded. The Chinese retaliated in 1521 by sending a fleet of junks to the Portuguese settlement and attacking them. The Portuguese were killed in the region or retreated to non-Chinese ports. The Chinese then issued a policy prohibiting anyone with European characteristics from entering Guangzhou or Guangdong.

The Portuguese would have completely lost their foothold in China were it not for the corruption and bribery that saturated the administrative system in Guangzhou (Smith 1920: 9). Despite the laws and regulations regarding dealings with foreigners, by 1537 three settlements had been established in the nearby region: Shang-chuan, Lang-peh-kao (Lampaçao), and Macau, which was established entirely on lies told to the Chinese. The Portuguese had told officials that tribute to the Chinese (which was in fact normal trading goods) had become wrecked in storms and needed to be dried. The Portuguese were allowed to erect sheds and structures for this purpose at Macau, but numerous merchants established themselves as tenants there and managed to pay the Chinese a yearly rent of 500 ounces of silver.

The location of Macau was beneficial and strategically chosen by the Portuguese, as it was in close communication with Guangzhou and connected via a river system. In contrast to their earlier dealings with the Chinese, the Portuguese attempted to appear more humble and comply with the wishes of the Chinese rather than with force. As it turned out, the policy, in conjunction with increased European activities in the region, would help the Portuguese Empire hold on to Macau even as its fortunes dwindled everywhere else across the world.

Portuguese Macau: The History and Legacy of the Autonomous Chinese Territory that Became the Last European Colony in Asia examines how this tiny foothold managed to last as a European possession for so long, and the dynamics that led to China establishing sovereignty over it at the end of the 20th century. Along with pictures depicting important people, places, and events, you will learn about Macau like never before.

Ancient and Medieval Trade

Trade between the Chinese and the rest of the world has a long and complex history. While in the 21st century it would be difficult to find commodities in a store that did not contain the label "Made in China" with the implication in some cases being that the goods are of lower quality (Urban Dictionary), this was not always the case and trade between China and the West has even resulted in the acculturation of Chinese goods. For example, in England, tea is considered to be a traditional English drink and has been incorporated into English culture while gunpowder has been adopted by cultures around the world.

It is believed that the first Western culture to initiate contact with the Chinese dates back to the Greeks of the 3rd century BCE. The Greeks apparently expanded into the area of the Tarim Basin of northwest China - while there are historical sources from Greeks such as Strabo, there is also some archaeological evidence suggesting a Greek presence in the region. In the mid-1980s, archaeologists working in the Shanpula (located in the Tarim Basin) burial ground came across a pair of pants with a unique pattern. The pants were in fact made from a tapestry that possibly depicted a "Greco-Scythian king with his spear and the centaur Chiron playing the trumpet, wearing the causia (large Greco-Macedonian hat) and covered with a lion skin..." (Christopoulos 2012: 15). These two images may also have been symbolic representations of Alexander the Great, who claimed to be a descendant of the mythical Achilles (represented by Chiron) and Heracles (represented by the lion skin).

The presence of the Greeks in the region could also be found on a molecular level in the mitochondrial DNA (mtDNA) from the burials at Shanpula. In 2007, researchers Xie Chengzhi *et al* found that the burial grounds were in use between 217 BCE and 283 CE (based on carbon-14 dating), and that the mtDNA "distribution showed that the ancient Sampula was a complex population with both European and Asian characteristics." This would be consistent with the histories that record that Alexander the Great married a Bactrian woman (a local from north of the Hindu-Kush region) and arranged for his generals to also marry local women (Holt 1989: 100).

Centuries later, the Roman Empire would take an interest in the goods of the Chinese, especially the silk. When Roman merchants began bringing gifts and offerings to the Han court in the 2nd century CE, the Chinese had already been manufacturing silk for more than 2,500 years. Archaeological evidence for sericulture, also known as silk farming, and the systematic use of the silkworm for silk comes from a ceramic vessel that was designed to represent the silkworm (Silberman 2012: 188). While the Romans were interested in the Chinese silk, it appears that there was some initial interest in Western goods, particularly in Southeast Asia where more non-organic Roman goods have been uncovered. In the ancient city of Óc Eo, in modern day Vietnam, gold medallions from the Roman Empire have been uncovered that were made during the reign of Antoninus Pius (r. CE 138-161) (Higham 2014).

It was also around this time that Chinese histories begin to record offerings from the Romans. In the *Hou Han-Shou* (Annals of the Later Han Dynasty covering CE 23-220) it is recorded that in 166 CE, an embassy from *Ta-ch'in* traveled from *Annam* (Vietnam) with gifts. *Ta-ch'in* is believed to have been the Chinese name for the Roman East, while the name that the emissaries claimed to represent was *An-tun*, a Chinese version of Antonius for the Roman Emperor Marcus Aurelius Antoninus Augustus (r. 161-180) (Young 2001).

Due to the difficulty of obtaining silk during this period, it was extremely expensive for the Romans to obtain the product. Pliny the Elder, a historian of the 1st century CE, wrote, "India, China and the Arabian Peninsula take one hundred million *sesterces* (Roman coinage) from our empire per annum at a conservative estimate: that is what our luxuries and women cost us." (Pliny 12.41.84).

The Romans eventually learned how the silk was made and became capable of making their own. According to Pliny the Elder, "Pamphile, a woman of Cos, the daughter of Platea, was the first person who discovered the art of unravelling these webs and spinning a tissue therefrom; indeed, she ought not to be deprived of the glory of having discovered the art of making vestments which, while they cover a woman, at the same moment reveal her naked charms." However, this silk was always inferior to the silk produced by the Chinese, who had perfected it over thousands of years.

The Roman Empire, as noted by Pliny, had to pay for this silk mainly by trading gold coins. Although there was some trade in other goods, such as glassware, the Chinese also were capable of producing glassware and therefore did not demand as much of it as the Romans demanded silk. In fact, this kind of trade imbalance, which saw Western Europeans crave Chinese goods more than the Chinese wanted Western goods, would play a significant role in the exchange of Chinese goods for most of the next 2,000 years. The imbalance came about in part because the royal Chinese courts viewed their culture as superior to all other cultures, and as such the Chinese court did not demand goods from inferior cultures. Furthermore, to the Chinese, inferior cultures were lucky for the opportunity to trade with the Chinese, a privilege which could be taken away or strictly controlled by the royal court. As a result, the Chinese had the advantage in trade negotiations and could demand gold and other precious metals from foreign empires in exchange for Chinese goods. In the modern era, this would compel the Europeans to pay massive amounts of silver for Chinese tea.

Trade between the East and the West continued sporadically and led to the development of a trade network known as the Silk Road stretching from the eastern coast of China to the Mediterranean coast. Given the vast distance that this trade route covered, the flow of goods was subject to the numerous empires and territories that the caravans had to cross. When wars erupted between nomadic tribes or empires, trade would become more irregular, thereby decreasing the quantity of a product (like silk) and increasing the demand for it.

Conflicts were particularly common between empires in the Middle East and the empires established by the Greeks and Romans. By the 4th century CE the Roman Empire had become destabilized due to poor economics, a lack of resources and spreading the Empire too thinly making control difficult. Replacing the Roman Empire was the Byzantine Empire. In the 6th century, Emperor Justinian I (r. CE 527-565) had begun to conquer and expand the Byzantine Empire; retaking much of the former Roman Empire.

The conflicts and expansion, however, interrupted the Silk Road trading routes for the Byzantine Empire, resulting in the Byzantines having to look for alternative options to obtain silk. Since the source of silk, the silkworm, had long been known, it seemed that the simplest way to obtain Chinese silk on a regular and more economical basis would be to import the silkworm to the West. The Chinese were well aware of this and had made it illegal to export the silkworm. Therefore, Justinian the Great secretly dispatched two monks in 552 to obtain silkworms for the empire. Over the course of two years, the monks traveled to China and managed to smuggle out silkworms and bring them to the Byzantine Empire (Hunt 2012).

A contemporary mosaic of Byzantine Emperor Justinian the Great

The expedition was a success for the Byzantine Empire and gave the empire control over the silk trade in Europe. Indeed, the establishment of silk factories in the Byzantine Empire would help support the economy for the next six centuries, but despite this supply of silk being supplied from Eurasia, the demand for Chinese silk never really ceased. This was due to the fact that the supplies available from production centers, like the Byzantine Empire, still could not meet the demands of the rest of the West, and the production quality was still inferior to that of the Chinese.

The Arrival of the Europeans

By the mid-15th century the Byzantine Empire had collapsed and the various Crusades that had taken place in the region had largely disrupted the overland routes of the Silk Road and trade. Compounding the difficulties of trade was the rise of the Ottoman Empire in place of the Byzantines and the outbreak of the Black Death in Europe.

It was roughly around this time that a period of European exploration began, and major factors that contributed to this period of exploration were introduced by the Chinese, albeit indirectly. The magnetic compass had already been developed and used by the Chinese sailors since the 12th century, although it had first been created in the 3rd century BCE as a divination device. The Song Dynasty then began using the device for land navigation in the 11th century and sailors began using it shortly after. The technology slowly spread west via Arab traders, although a case can be made for the independent European creation for the compass (Southey 1812: 210). Regardless, by the 13th century the compass had found its way to Western traders, coming at a time that trade had been increasing across Europe.

Trade was able to increase in Europe around the world due to more effective ships being introduced, and some of the improvements that were made to the ships were first introduced by the Chinese. The introduction of multiple mast ships and the sternpost rudders allowed the ships to travel quicker and be more maneuverable. By the 14th century, ships were now much larger and able to support long distance travel with a minimum number of crew aboard.

At this time in China, the empire was going through a transition from the Mongol dynasty to the Ming dynasty. Although the Mongols had established successful trade routes between the East and the West and provided a fair amount of protection for the caravans, the Han Chinese people suffered overtaxation and discrimination under their rule. This contributed toward a series of rebellions in the mid-14th century, with the Mongols being overthrown in 1368.

Once again, the Han ruled China, and as is typical of successful rebellions, the practices of the previous government were radically changed. Trade between the newly established Great Ming Empire and the foreigners was deemed illegal, with the exception of specific trade delegations and officials. This practice happened again after the first emperor, Hongwu, died.

The emperor named his grandson, Zhu Yunwen as his successor, but Zhu Di (a son of Hongwu) disagreed with this decision. Zhu Di successfully rebelled against the Jianwen Emperor (the royal name of Zhu Yunwen) and became the Yongle Emperor. The Yongle Emperor then proceeded to overturn his father's proclamations, which were decrees overturning Mongol laws.

The Yongle Emperor

In tandem with these moves, the Yongle Emperor established a large naval fleet so that China could begin establishing trade connections with other empires. This would be done through the *Xiafan Guanjun* (foreign expeditionary armada) led by Admiral Zheng He (also written Cheng Ho) (Arnold 2002: 7). The fleet would bear gifts and treasures as tributary for other kingdoms. This maneuver was likely in order for the new emperor to obtain a legitimate standing in the eyes of other lands since he had technically overthrown the legitimate emperor. These voyages were not typically trade or merchant voyages, however. Upon offering tribute to other kingdoms, the

11

Ming court expected tribute in return, especially in the form of luxuries and curiosities. In other words, the goods brought back were not necessarily items that would be beneficial to the Ming court or Han people in general, but were foreign curiosities such as giraffes, lions, camels, bobcats and African ivory (Tsai 2001: 206).

The first of seven voyages that the fleet took began in 1405. The goal of the voyage was to establish favorable relations with distant lands, and with the fleet came 27,000 troops and goods. The fleet sailed to Champa, Java and all the way to Ceylon and the southern tip of the Indian peninsula before turning back to return to China. The trip was largely seen as a success, and shortly after envoys from the foreign lands the fleet had visited arrived in China bearing tribute and homage.

By the end of the sixth expedition, the Yongle Emperor had died and was succeeded by Zhu Gaozhi, who assumed the name Hongxi as emperor. Hongxi did not view the expeditions favorably and ordered that the fleets cease all diplomatic expeditions. The final voyage would not take place until after the death of Hongxi, who was replaced by the Xuande Emperor. In 1431, the fleet left and sailed for the Indian Ocean, making stops at the kingdoms of insular Southeast Asia along the way. The result of the seven voyages was that China had established itself with other major powers as a formidable force that needed to be recognized. Although the fleet was largely a treasure fleet with diplomatic intentions, it was also largely a military fleet that sought to intimidate the foreigners.

In fact, the military contingent that made up the fleet would also help combat the pirates and illicit trade that had begun developing in the southern waters by Guangdong. The Japanese had also taken to piracy along these southern coasts, and although Admiral Zheng He did not actively attempt to eliminate the threat of pirates in these regions, this huge naval force did manage to inspire terror to anyone who laid eyes on it, whether pirate or a foreign port. There were several instances of pirates attempting to capture treasure ships; however, Zheng He laid waste to these pirates and essentially secured the maritime routes for trade.

China had become economically and technologically advanced compared to civilizations in Europe at the time, and the fleet, which had reached a total of 3,500 ships, was unmatched by any other world power. Nevertheless, the fleet never made an eighth voyage, and the ships were either burned in the docks or left to rot. Xuande believed that the tributes that were being sent to him and China were unnecessary and were being carried out on behalf of his grandfather's wishes rather than his own. In the end, Xuande sided with his father's belief that the voyages should cease. Xuande felt that the policies established by the Hongwu Emperor were more in line with the way the empire should be run, and so China began to revert to the xenophobic policies of Hongwu and reduce its presence in other lands. By 1525, the largest naval fleet in the world had essentially been destroyed or dismantled by China itself. On top of that, the records and maps of Zheng He were confiscated by the Ministry of War in 1477.

Upon the death of the Yongle Emperor the tributary fleets ceased and in 1433 the Ming court began to isolate itself from the outside world. The Ming court reestablished the Haijin policies, sea bans that were initially meant to disrupt Japanese piracy that had been plaguing the coasts of China. This policy forbade trade with foreigners, especially over the waterways, with the exception of official tributes which post-Yongle emperors were less inclined to take up. This put a large strain on the coastal villages and the economy in general as the court and merchants were not able to generate profits from the taxation of imports. As a result, the coasts of China became less loyal to the Ming court and officials of these coastal regions could easily be bribed by foreign merchants.

While the Yongle Emperor was sending tributary ships across the Indian Ocean as far as the eastern coast of Africa between 1405 and 1433, the Portuguese were exploring the West coast of Africa and the Atlantic under orders from Prince Henry the Navigator. At this point, Europeans had not yet been capable of navigating completely around Africa; the ships being built were not yet fully capable of being able to sail very far from the coast and navigation in open waters was difficult. However, the Portuguese continued pushing down the western African coast looking for ways to bypass the Ottomans and Muslims of Africa who had been making overland trade routes difficult. In 1451, Prince Henry the Navigator helped fund and develop a new type of ship, the caravel, that featured triangular lateen sails which would be able to travel in the open ocean and sail against the wind. In 1488, Bartholomew Diaz rounded the southern tip of Africa, named the Cape of Good Hope by King John of Portugal, and entered the Indian Ocean from the Atlantic.

Henry the Navigator

One explorer, Christopher Columbus, sought funding from the Portuguese to search for a passage to Asia by sailing westwards, but he was rejected. At this time in the late 15th century, Portugal's domination of the western African sea routes prompted the neighboring Crown of Castile and the Catholic monarchs in modern Spain to search for an alternative route to south and east Asia (termed *Indies*), so they provided Columbus with the funding he required. Ultimately, Columbus discovered the Americas in 1492, and Spanish settlements in the "West Indies" would eventually be established.

Of course, when it became clear Columbus hadn't landed in Asia, it was understood by everyone that this was not necessarily the route the Europeans were searching for, and the Portuguese continued to send explorers around the Cape of Good Hope in an attempt to reach the East Indies. After a two-year voyage, in 1499, Vasco da Gama had successfully reached India and returned to Portugal.

A portrait believed to depict Vasco da Gama

The Portuguese had found access to the trade regions that they had been searching for, but sailing from Portugal to India and beyond would require too many resources to travel with at once. To remedy this problem, Portugal began establishing a number of forts and trading posts along the route. The Portuguese were able to establish a fort on the west coast of India, Fort Manuel, in 1500, and in 1505 a fort was erected off the coast of Tanzania, thus beginning a trend of European colonization in Africa and Asia that would last for the next 400 years.

The presence of the Portuguese in India was a disturbance to the Muslim merchants which resulted in hostilities against Portuguese merchant ships in the Indian Ocean. The Portuguese had also managed to gain control of the mouth of the Red Sea and the Persian Gulf, allowing them to control the sea routes from the Mediterranean to India. The Muslims of the region could not compete with the Portuguese ships and sought allies in their struggle. The Ottoman Empire answered the call of the Muslims in India and Africa, thus beginning the Portuguese-Ottoman War.

While the struggle with the Ottomans dominated the Indian Ocean, the Portuguese continued their eastward expansion to East Asia and took control of strategic trade routes there, just as they had done with the Red Sea and Persian Gulf. Alfonso de Albuquerque was charged with this task, and he selected Malacca as a strategic location to capture which would, in his mind, cripple the Muslim spice trade in the region and severely weaken Cairo and Mecca. In 1511, Albuquerque arrived with an armada and began to bombard the city after failing to come to terms with the Sultan. Some Hindu and Chinese residents of the city offered their help to the Portuguese by providing barges for him to land his troops, but supposedly, Albuquerque did not want the Chinese to be punished for helping the Portuguese and thus allowed them to stay on the Portuguese ships or to set sail. After weeks of fighting and assault, the Sultan retreated from the city and the Portuguese were able to capture Malacca and control the straits there.

Albuquerque

The foothold of Malacca would act as another Portuguese stepping stone on their way to China. From there, the Portuguese ships could gather supplies and forces to proceed to mainland Southeast Asia and China.

Tense Relations

While the Portuguese had accomplished disrupting the spice trade of the Muslims and Ottoman Empire by controlling the Straits of Malacca, they had also, unknowingly, attacked one of the tributaries of China. As a result, the early reports that the Chinese had of the foreigners was that they possessed violent tendencies and would use them to occupy lands (Brinkley 1904: 170).

The first ships sent to southern China by Albuquerque were led by Jorge Álvares in 1513, and they were able to dock at Lintin Island near present day Hong Kong and Guangzhou. Principal trading would take place at the port of Tamou in Hau Chuen (also known as San-shan, Shangchuan, Tamou or Saint John Island) and would act as the port of trade between Malacca and Guangzhou. Upon returning successfully after initiating first contact between the two cultures, Rafael Perestrello was dispatched to establish trade relations with the Ming court. Between 1513 and 1516, Perestrello made several voyages to the Guangdong province and was eventually received well by the merchants of Guangzhou (later referred to as Canton by the English). The general acceptance of the Portuguese merchants was taken as a sign that more ships could be sent to the region for trade.

Nine vessels were dispatched in total, five ships and four junks, to southern China under the command of Perez de Andrade (Jesus 1902: 3). The new ships were viewed skeptically by the Ming officials, however. What must be kept in mind was the trading philosophy and view that the Chinese had at the time. Trade was a privilege that the Ming court was generous enough to allow for the barbarian foreigners, and trade should be dictated by government officials rather than merchants who had no official ties to the government. This notion, coupled with the rather ominous (from the point of view of the Chinese) Portuguese takeover of Malacca, as well as the arrival of nine Portuguese ships, was a cause for concern. Andrade worked hard to dispel any idea of hostilities on the part of the Portuguese and was eventually allowed to send two of his ships up the river to Guangzhou. So successful were his actions with the Chinese that some of his vessels were accompanied up the coast to establish factories (merchant warehouses) at Ningpo and Tsuanchou.

The successful merchant ties created by Andrade would be short-lived. In 1518, the brother of Andrade, Simon (Simão), arrived and established a colony on Tamou Island near Macau. While the port and island were already established to allow trade between the two cultures, Simon proceeded to establish a fort on the island. He had declared that this was necessary in order to protect the island and region from pirates. In order to deter piracy, gallows were also erected nearby where a delinquent was executed in Portuguese fashion. The problem with these actions, in the eyes of the Chinese, was that the Portuguese were enforcing their own laws on Chinese land and establishing Portuguese sovereignty. This prompted a wave of xenophobia among the Chinese population and began a wave of hatred for the foreigners. Rumors of the malicious deeds of Simon were spread, including that Simon had the children of noble families in Guangzhou kidnapped so that he might eat them (Jesus 1902: 5). The exact actions of Simon during this period are not completely known, but Simon was clearly carrying out his own actions with little input from the other Portuguese officials.

This became particularly problematic upon the death of the Ming Emperor in 1521. The Chinese officials claimed that due to the death of the emperor, the foreigners must vacate Chinese lands. The new emperor subsequently took the Portuguese emissaries hostage in exchange for the surrender of Malacca, but the Portuguese refused to leave and fortified themselves on Tamou. Those Portuguese merchants who attempted to sail to Guangzhou and commence trade were arrested.

Despite 50 Chinese junks attempting to prevent merchant vessels from docking at Tamou, the Chinese were cautious not to come too close to the defended settlement. The Portuguese, however, were outmanned, and after a 40 day siege, the Portuguese dispatched three ships to meet the Chinese fleet. The ships briefly skirmished with the imperial vessels before a storm offered the Portuguese a chance to retreat to Malacca. The hostages that the Chinese authorities held were never returned, and only years later did the letters of these Portuguese officials reach home describing their treatment (Jesus 1902: 8-9).

The Portuguese continued to hold onto Tamou in order to keep some sort of presence in China, and an envoy led by Martim Afonso de Mello Coutinho was sent to maintain this. He was under orders to establish a fort, either at Tamou or another strategic location, with him in command and garrisoned by his crew. In August 1522, they arrived in Tamou, but they were swiftly set upon by the imperial fleet. The encounter was disastrous for the Portuguese, and during the retreat one of their vessels caught fire and exploded, causing many survivors to be cast out into the water. Another Portuguese vessel attempted to rescue the survivors from the sea, but it was set upon by the Chinese. The crew of these vessels were captured and starved or tortured to death. The rest of the Portuguese fleet fled to Malacca.

Unlike in the rest of the world, where the Portuguese were frequently dealing with wars, battles, and rebellions, in China the Portuguese were never able to bring their full military might to avenge these losses. Due to so many other conflicts in other parts of the world, the naval fleet could not be drawn so far away or else the Portuguese forces would be spread too thin. Thus, eventually, the frequent military failures in China caused the Portuguese to abandon the idea of a military fort in the region altogether. If the Portuguese were to have a role in China, it could not be through force, but the lack of military or state support did little to dissuade the merchants who were drawn to the profits that China could still offer.

The suspicions that the Chinese had of the foreigners never went away and were only fueled as other European empires came into contact with China. The Spanish, for example, had been paying for Chinese exports with silver from the New World (mainly Mexico) through their base in Manila. The Chinese believed that this silver must have come from Manila and the Chinese population in the Philippines began looking for the source of the valuable metals. Suspicion from the Spaniards reached a breaking point in 1603 when they massacred all of the Chinese on the islands. Furthermore, whenever a Chinese merchant vessel came to trade in the islands, the number of Chinese people was limited, and they were heavily taxed.

Between 1635 and 1637, a fleet of four ships from the British Empire reached Macau under the command of Captain John Weddell. The captain's dealings with the Portuguese were hindered since they saw the English as commercial rivals, so Weddell brought his fleet to nearby Guangzhou. Although Weddell had made his peaceful intentions clear, the Portuguese had secretly been feeding the Chinese authorities misinformation as to the intents of the new foreigners. The result was a brief exchange of cannon fire and raiding between the two sides. After the exchange of gunfire and raiding, the Chinese agreed that the cargoes of the ships could be sold. The merchants who had accompanied Weddell felt that future hostilities should be avoided and that it would be far easier to pay off the officials of Guangzhou; in their minds, any money lost from the bribes would quickly be made back through trade (Smith 1920: 11).

Needless to say, not all of the English merchants were fully convinced that trade with the Chinese was worth the effort, and another trading fleet from the British would not reach China until 1664. Even then, unfortunately for the British, the Portuguese again convinced the Chinese that the British were thieves and violent people, resulting in poor trading opportunities for the East India Company (Brinkley 1904: 188-189). Concerning the actions by the Portuguese, Sir John Davis, second Governor of Hong Kong, wrote, "In the progress of all these trials one of the most striking circumstances is the stupid pertinacity with which the Portuguese at Macao excluded English ships from that port, and the perfidy with which they represented their supposed rivals to the Chinese with a view to prevent their getting a footing at Canton.... Their systematic policy has been to attribute motives to the English which should injure them with the provincial Government." (Brinkley 1904: 192).

Even in the 19th century, this Portuguese influence had an impact on China's dealings with other Europeans. In 1845 the governor of Hong Kong, Sir John Davis, would write, [The Portuguese] conduct was not calculated to impress the Chinese with any favorable idea of Europeans; and when, in course of time, they came to be competitors with the Dutch and the English, the contest of mercantile avarice tended to place them all in a still worse point of view. To this day the character of the Europeans is represented as that of a race of men intent alone on the gains of commercial traffic and regardless altogether of the means of attainment. Struck by the perpetual hostilities which existed among the foreign adventurers, assimilated in other respects by a close resemblance in their costumes and manners, the Government of the country became disposed to treat them with a degree of jealousy and exclusion which it had not deemed necessary to be exercised towards the more peaceable and well-ordered Arabs, their predecessors (Brinkley 1904: 175).

The Establishment of Portuguese Macau

Portuguese merchants switched to a different approach and attempted to bribe their way into creating settlements in China. The settlements Liampo and Chincheo were established through such means, but these settlements lasted only a few years before everyone in them was murdered. They were prohibited from traveling to Guangzhou under punishment of torture and death, forcing many of the merchants to set up simple tents using sails on the shore to conduct quick business and then leave. It was not until 1537 that the Chinese, through bribery and conciliation, allowed foreign trade on the island of Lampaçao (or Lang-peh-kau), Shangchuan, and Macau (Brinkley 1904: 174). The Portuguese were allowed to settle there and were allowed, unofficially, to conduct business in Guangzhou. On Lampaçao, the Portuguese population

19

quickly rose to around 500 and trade centered mainly on pepper from their other colonies in exchange for silk and musk.

The establishment at Macau, which is a Portuguese abbreviation for the Chinese name "Ama-kau," or Harbor of Ama, was done through deception. The location was strategic because it is located on the southern portion of the Pearl River's estuary, thereby allowing access to both the sea and a direct connection to Guangzhou. Portuguese merchants had stranded a ship they claimed to be carrying tribute after a storm, after which they claimed that the goods must be dried and pleaded with Chinese officials to allow them to construct sheds at Macau to salvage the goods. The Portuguese, in the end, ended up paying a yearly rent of silver in exchange for staying at Macau.

It is questionable as to what year this exactly took place since the Chinese accounts give various dates (Jesus 1902: 17). In the *Chronicle of Heang-shan*, the author states that in 1553 the Portuguese vessels had been struck by a typhoon and their tribute was damaged by water (in Rémusat 1829: 328-329).

Regardless, the mid-16th century witnessed the beginning of a new era of trade relations between the Portuguese and the Chinese, and this is thought to have been due to the numerous Japanese pirates that plagued the coast. In 1557, the Portuguese fleet was able to attack and drive away a large force of pirates around Macau. This act was recognized by the Chinese emperor, who, according to the Portuguese, allowed them official sanction at Macau. Like the Chinese accounts that offer conflicting dates, this account too is not recorded - the official documents are missing and the stone upon which this edict was carved has gone missing.

Another account from the Colonial Office of Lisbon offers a similar account, but it differs in one major regard. According to the Colonial Office, "The China Sea was infested by pirates and insurgents who wrought havoc on the trade and shipping, when, after due preparation, the Portuguese assailed the marauders, and soon cleared the sea of the scourge, much to the relief and joy of the Chinese. The Portuguese then bore down upon Heang-shan, where large tracts were held by a powerful chieftain. After staunch resistance, he was vanquished, and the island taken, by vassals of the crown of Portugal; when it results that the sovereignty in question is founded on the right of conquest, acquired by the arms of Portugal, and at the cost of Portuguese blood. The island occupied, and Macau being best adapted for trading purposes, the city was built on that peninsula. This the Chinese would certainly not have permitted unless they fully recognized the Portuguese rights over that territory. Nor would the Portuguese have incurred the heavy outlay they did in building the city, had they not been quite sure of their rights to do so independently of the laws and government of China." (Parker 1890). In such a case, the Portuguese essentially claimed that the lands were inhabited by pirates and when the Portuguese fought and conquered these pirates, they had a right to the land that the pirates were inhabiting, under the concept that "sovereignty …is founded on the right of conquest."

It is likely that China's assent to the Portuguese residing and trading in the region is a combination of all of the accounts. The Chinese have long had a history of not recounting events in the most objective way, tending to favor the role and accomplishments of the Chinese over the actions of foreigners. Rather than have the emperor acknowledge the Portuguese right of conquest, it would seem more favorable if the emperor granted the land to the foreigners, thereby presenting the Chinese court in control of the situation while extolling the generosity of the emperor.

Whatever the case may be, it is generally agreed upon historically that by 1557 the Portuguese were developing Macau into a more European-styled settlement without interference from the Chinese court. The Portuguese were ruling using European laws and even had rights to the land of the conquered Heang-shan tracts which provided Macau with food. With such an establishment, the Portuguese at Macau were able to operate independently of the Chinese altogether.

The early population of the colony was approximately 500, with a mixture of Portuguese men with Japanese and Malaccan wives, their children, and a mixture of other Malaccans, Indians, and Africans who were mainly brought over for slave labor. Largely absent from the colony were Chinese populations. The Chinese were allowed into the colony, but only on the condition that they did not settle on the land. In other words, the skilled laborers who were allowed to work in the colony would need to leave the colony at the end of each day.

The early government of the colony was largely controlled by the commodore of the royal fleet that frequently made port there on its way to and from Japan. Supporting the commodore was an appointed judge and elected merchants that made up a special council. The makeup of the council being dominantly merchants demonstrates that the Portuguese had learned from their past mistakes in establishing colonies with the intent of using force. Instead, they now decided to focus on trade as a means to rule the actions of the colony.

The merchants were far more interested in profit and trading than in conquest, which frequently resulted in a disruption of trade and, as happened in the past, a loss of their foothold in China. By 1573, the farming of Heang-shan had come to an end through the force of the local mandarins, or Chinese lords, and the Portuguese colony was forced to depend on the Chinese for subsistence. This put the young colony in a vulnerable position since the Chinese would now be able to cut off the colony from food whenever they wanted. In essence, the Portuguese would need to be subservient to the Chinese lords of the region. The farming land of Heang-shan was easily taken from the Portuguese, and at the same time a wall was constructed between the peninsula of Macau and mainland China. Now the Portuguese were isolated in their colony and could only travel outside the wall with a Chinese-issued passport.

Occasionally, the gate of the erected wall, known as Porta do Cerco to the Portuguese, would be opened so that provisions could be allowed in. When the gate was sealed, a series of papers would be placed across the gate reading in Chinese: "Dread our greatness, and respect our virtue." Surrounding the wall were Chinese troops who were more mercenaries than trained soldiers. The mercenaries would take the occasions of the opening of the gate to harass any of the suppliers to the point that they were actually flogged in Macau for their actions. Unfortunately, these retaliations would be met with a shortage of food for Macau for a time, causing a portion of the lower class to starve to death.

The Porta do Cerco in 1890

Over the next decade, the 500 taels of silver that the Portuguese had been paying as a bribe for annual rent (which the Portuguese looked at as tribute) evolved into a solidified official rent payment to the Chinese. This was seen as a step back for the Portuguese because the payment of rent essentially did away with their claim to sovereignty through conquest, whereas when they were paying tribute, they saw it as paying the local government protection money (as was done in other colonies). Soon, other authorities were interested in extracting payments from the Portuguese, and in 1582, a newly appointed viceroyalty of Guangzhou demanded a meeting with the major authorities of Macau so that they might explain what right the colony had to govern itself. The viceroyalty of Guangzhou, of course, was blatantly ignoring the proclamation of the emperor, which surely would have been known to the authorities.

The principal civil, legal, and ecclesiastical authorities that who summoned were skeptical of the request, but they knew that some form of action needed to be done in order to not upset the ruler. Therefore, a legal functionary named Penella and two Italian Jesuits were sent bearing presents such as silk and crystals. Fortunately, they and the gifts were well received and the viceroy decided to pay for the gifts, but only under the condition that the money they received be used to provide him with more gifts. Situations such as this were typical of the relationship between the Portuguese colony and the rest of China. They could not invoke their right through conquest, because to do so would mean to cut them off from all supplies, and if they denied the surrounding Chinese lords and authorities, they would be cut off from all supplies. The best that the Portuguese in Macau could do was appease the Chinese in any way possible and not upset the authorities.

In that same year, news of the 1580 usurpation of the crown of Portugal by Philip II of Spain reached Macau, and the colony had little choice but to acknowledge and swear allegiance to the Castilian sovereign. However, not all residents of Macau were satisfied with this union and actions were taken in 1583 to make Macau more independent from Spain. Led by Bishop Belchior Carneiro, a senatorial administration was established based on earlier governing techniques. The election process was to be triennial, with every resident of Macau given a vote, and six electors would be chosen and sworn into office. The revenue for the colony was to be based solely on that which was derived from customs. An entire system had been established by the people of Macau and was given some recognition by the Portuguese viceroy of India, Dom Duarte de Menezes, but the Spanish king nevertheless insisted on appointing a chief-justice administrator. The king dispatched a number of chief-justice administrators, but these were largely ignored by the senate. So much so was the chief-justice administrator rendered useless that the position was eventually abolished entirely and the position was assigned to the senatorial senior alderman instead. This was seen as a major victory for the autonomy of Macau and the senate.

Philip II

The senate was now forced, as the leading authority of the colony, to deal with the surrounding Chinese authorities who would often initiate quarrels with the Portuguese. For example, a surrounding Chinese lord would dispatch a messenger stating some grievance, whether real or imagined, that the senate would need to handle. Typically, the situation would go one of two ways, the senate would agree to pay the messenger or send tribute to satisfy the lord, or they would attempt some other way to appease the lord. In the case of the latter, however, there was always the possibility that provisions to the colony would be cut off for a time thereby creating internal problems for the colony and could ultimately lead to death through starvation. Thus, the senate would more than likely always be forced to pay the surrounding Chinese lords.

Despite these high costs, the Portuguese colony began to become more profitable as the colonies in India began to deteriorate and the Spanish of Manila had to trade through Macau without having direct access to China itself. Additionally, Macau was a center of trade with Japan, which was interested in goods like wines, cotton, and raw silk. In exchange for these goods, Japan would generally pay in gold bullion. This bullion, in turn, could be used for the purchase of Chinese goods (since the Chinese did not desire European or the goods of other barbarian cultures), which could then be sold to the Spanish or other Europeans.

In short order, trade relations with the Chinese became more favorable, with the Chinese offering the Portuguese better deals on import duties and services. As a result of this successful trade ring, Lisbon became a major economical center of goods, which it presented to the rest of Europe in competition with Venice.

The Dutch

However, just as the trade of the Silk Road in the past was influenced by the conflicts of nomads, warlords, and the shifting powers of kingdoms, so too was Macau's trade influenced by conflicts in Europe. Between 1568 and 1648, the Spanish Empire would struggle with rebellions and revolts in the Netherlands. The rise of Protestantism in the Netherlands had become a problem for the Roman Catholic Spanish Empire, which had begun taking measures to suppress the religious point of view. Charles V had begun the Inquisition of the Netherlands in an attempt to make Catholicism the main religion of the region, but when Philip II succeeded his father, he enacted particularly heavy taxation and stepped up the suppression of Protestantism in the region. As a result of the conflicts and revolts in the Netherlands, Philip II placed an embargo on the exchange of Chinese goods with the Netherlands.

With the Netherlands no longer able to obtain Chinese goods from Portugal, they were forced to look for alternative routes to China. Expeditions were sent to look for a route via the Arctic, and though these attempts failed, soon the Dutch would make their own way to China.

According to the *Chinese Repository*, the first encounter with these red-haired, blue-eyed tribute-bearers frightened the people (1832: 370). The Dutch, however, were completely unaware of the extent of contact that the Portuguese had with the Chinese, or the long history that had taken place for the Portuguese to gain some form of favor with the Chinese. To Dutch eyes, the Portuguese had established a colony on China and that was sufficient reason enough for the Dutch to do the same. Moreover, the Dutch arrived in full force with the intention of assuming control of land to establish a colony or to drive the Portuguese out of Macau and take control of that territory.

The Dutch fleet, led by Admiral Jacob van Neck, arrived in the waters of Macau in 1601. This would be the third voyage to the East Indies that the celebrated Dutch admiral would make, and along the way he engaged the Portuguese at Ternate in Indonesia. However, the Dutch fleet was unable to secure Macau at this time, despite the unfortified nature of the colony. In 1603, a minor skirmish took place between the two empires, with the Dutch opening fire on Macau and looting a ship before retreating. During these hostilities and the tense standoff, the Portuguese were using their good standing with the Chinese in order to influence their perception of the Dutch. Thus, by 1604, the Dutch had still been unsuccessful in forcing themselves into the Chinese trade market.

Dutch Admiral van Waerwijk was sent to continue hostilities against Macau but was driven off due to a typhoon forcing him to retreat to India. The Dutch then took mainly to piracy and attacking Portuguese trade ships in the East Indies. It became clear to the authorities of Macau that fortifications were needed in order to keep their colony, but this was extremely problematic for the Chinese who, although on good terms with the Portuguese, did not trust the foreigners to not take more land via force. This worry involved the creation of forts and large standing military complexes, so much so that churches would sometimes be misidentified by the Chinese as forts (Jesus 1902: 58). This stemmed in part from the ceremonious creation of churches like St. Paul's. The church would be shielded from view of the public until the unveiling, and the workers hired for the project were dominantly Japanese. To the Chinese, this secretive construction being erected by the barbaric Europeans and the Japanese who had long pirated the nearby waterways could easily have been some sort of fortification.

A sketch of St. Paul's after it had been damaged by a fire in 1635

A modern picture of the Ruins of St. Paul's

One instance of mistaken building identity escalated into violence when a Jesuit wearing Chinese clothing was thought to have begun a campaign for emperor. At the time, there were a number of Chinese military leaders who had been converted by missionaries which made their political alliances suspect to the masses. It was believed that at any moment they might use their military following and strategic posts to overthrow the Chinese in the region. As a result of the Chinese dressed Jesuit being mistaken for a sign of the beginning of a coup, a mob attacked a church. The religiously zealous Portuguese rose up to counter this attack, driving the Chinese mob away and proceeded to attack a Chinese lord's manor. Peace was eventually restored through the combined efforts of the Chinese lord of Heang-shan and the Macau senate, but there were still simmering tensions between the two cultures.

Rumor had begun to spread among the Chinese that the Italian Jesuit missionary Lazzaro Cattaneo was planning on leading a Portuguese invasion of China to make himself emperor. Many of the misunderstandings from the previous riot were still in place, but Cattaneo seemed like a particularly interesting target for the Chinese. He had, first of all, been involved in the secretive building of St. Paul's, which was still skeptically viewed, and moreover, he was rumored to have traveled to Peking and versed himself well in Chinese ways. It was believed that his supposed travels were to secure a number of followers and learn the easiest means of travel so that he may quickly topple the emperor. This conspiracy was so thoroughly believed and circulated around Macau that it caused a mass panic and an exodus of the Chinese from the region to Guangzhou.

Upon arriving at Guangzhou, the Chinese refugees spread their fear of Cattaneo and the Portuguese to the Chinese lords, who quickly called out for military support. The city of Guangzhou and the surrounding waterways and borders were to be heavily guarded day and night. Furthermore, the inhabitants were restricted from housing anyone from Macau as it could be Cattaneo. Once these precautions were in place, a warning message was sent to the emperor in Peking.

Trade and provisions were stopped for Macau, and the senate of Macau was left struggling with how to deal with these absurd claims. From the point of view of the Portuguese, it seemed absurd that a handful of merchants would have any ambition to overthrow the entire empire. It is clear that at this point the Chinese court still had not fully grasped the value that trade in itself had to the Portuguese and the Europeans. Among the Chinese court, acts of tribute were more desired than that of trade, if at all. The Chinese view of their own culture was still that theirs was the superior one, which meant others would always want it.

Fears continued to fester in Guangzhou and an army was being prepared to lay siege to Macau. Ahead of the military, a viceroy of Guangzhou visited Macau in order to establish what the situation was in the colony. Cattaneo received the viceroy himself and gave him a tour of St. Paul's and other churches. Upon seeing the books and studying priests within the buildings, the viceroy was convinced that there were no military intentions from the merchants or priests of Macau. When the viceroy returned to Guangzhou, word was spread that the foreigners did not mean to overthrow the Ming dynasty or invade China. Peace and trade were gradually resumed in Macau, albeit more cautiously by the Chinese.

Tensions continued between the two cultures and any harassment by the Chinese was taken under the threat of starvation. In 1613 a series of new restrictions were imposed on the colony: no Japanese servants were to be brought to the colony; no Chinese subjects could be bought; no new housing without permission; and unmarried merchants must stay upon their ships. The people of Macau agreed to these new restrictions in order to continue trading with the empire. Nevertheless, fortifications were still required of the colony for protection against external threats such as the Dutch.

In 1615, it was ordered by the king that a fort or fortification be established in Macau. Officer Francisco Lopes Carrasco carried out the orders secretly and insisted to the Chinese authorities, when questioned, that they were for protection from pirates. He established a headquarters on Monte de São Paulo, a central height in Macau, where Jesuits assisted in the production of fortifications. The production of cannons and weapons at Macau were greatly boosted in 1621 when a Jesuit was sent to the emperor with three large cannons and a crew of artillery men. When these guns were used in the service of the emperor against rebels, who tended to attack in condensed clusters, the casualties and shock of the weapons drove back the attacking rebels. Pleased with the success of the weapons, the emperor took advantage of the Portuguese at Macau and ordered military rifles and cannons to be produced more regularly for the Chinese.

In fact, the Ming emperor allowed the training of a military force in Macau consisting of Chinese, local residents of Macau, and Portuguese. Approximately 400 musketeers were created in Macau and commanded by Pedro Cordeiro and Antonio Rodriguez del Campo. Once this force was established, it proceeded inland, via horseback and boats, towards Guangzhou for protection against a possible revolt. Although the military force was subsequently not needed and never reached its final destination, the Portuguese gained considerable favor with the emperor.

During this time, Macau was left largely undefended. Chinese pirates were well aware of the civil uprisings that were taking place inland, and with 400 musketeers being absent from the city, Macau would be vulnerable to attack. The pirates, however, underestimated the superior firepower and strength of the Portuguese ships. While attempting to take Macau as a base of operations, the pirates lost nearly 1,500 men and were driven off. The prestige of the Portuguese military had, by this point, spread to Southeast Asia, where the kingdom of Siam began employing Portuguese troops in the region.

The Dutch attempted again to take Macau by force in 1622. Originally the Dutch fleet was to be supported by two English vessels, but due to a miscommunication, the English fleet went to Japan instead. Nevertheless, the two remaining Dutch vessels tried for a surprise attack against the colony, but the people of Macau were able to resist the attack and the Dutch fleet retreated.

A large fleet returned later that year consisting of 13 ships. In face of such a force, Macau was nearly defenseless, with only 80 Europeans in the colony who were trained as musketeers. At the time, the 400 musketeers had yet to return from their march inland and other merchants were away at this time of year.

With a massive landing force of approximately 800 soldiers, the Dutch began their assault on Macau, but the artillery that had been established at the Jesuit fortification on the Monte began bombarding the advancing army, successfully hitting a gunpowder wagon. Such a loss of gunpowder greatly affected the Dutch, because while they had the numbers, their military might nevertheless depended on gunpowder to suppress and maintain control. The loss of the gunpowder wagon forced the Dutch commanders to alter their plans and greatly affected the morale of the Dutch troops.

As the Dutch advanced across the open plains towards the city, fortifications the Portuguese had placed on the surrounding high points allowed the Jesuits and the few military commanders available to anticipate and counter the Dutch forces. After the Dutch revised their attack following the loss of the gunpowder, they attempted to secure a high position and retreat from the open plains. With the advantageous viewpoint provided by the Monte, the Portuguese could see which high point was to be taken and counter the Dutch by securing it first. Despite being outnumbered, the Portuguese were able to drive the Dutch soldiers into a panic and caused many of them to flee to the sea. Furthermore, the Portuguese emancipated their black slave population who fiercely fought against the Dutch. After the battle, their bravery would be recognized and rewarded by the Chinese authorities with a distribution of extra provisions.

The casualty numbers for the Battle of Macau vary according to sources. Accounts written by the Portuguese place the number of Dutch casualties at around 800, while the Dutch, on the other hand, place the total number of casualties at only 136, with 126 wounded (Boxer 1948: 83-84). The discrepancy may be due to the fact that the Dutch were only counting European casualties and not those of the Japanese or other foreigners that were in the service of the Dutch during the battle. Regardless, the Portuguese suffered minimal casualties, although they did lose many of their high-ranking military commanders.

Other Problems in the 17th Century

The successful battle against the Dutch compelled the authorities in the Portuguese colony of Goa, India to recognize the importance Macau was playing in the struggle against the Dutch. In 1623, it called for an official governor to oversee Macau. Thus, in July of that year, Dom Francisco Mascarenhas arrived in Macau with a company of soldiers while 200 musketeers and several bombards arrived from the Philippines. Dom Francisco Mascarenhas was to have power over the military and jurisdiction over the courts, while the senate was to assist him in his governing. However, like the earlier military-governors who had been dispatched in the past, the people of Macau were not so willing to accept orders from a governor appointed by the Roman Catholic Castilian king. The entire time Macau was part of the greater Castilian Spanish empire, only the Portuguese flag would be flown. This was likely part of the local display of independence, but also part of the strict Chinese court's understanding of external affairs. To fly a different flag would mean dealing with a different, non-Portuguese power, something that would invite the Spanish into Chinese dealings, and that kind of confusion would be undesirable to both parties.

Dom Francisco Mascarenhas was adamant that his orders be heeded, which led to high tensions in Macau. It is believed that he was, nonetheless, able to have increased fortifications at Macau by bribing Chinese officials to turn a blind eye to his constructions. By 1623, Macau had finally established a formidable fortification, with the hermitage of Guia having been converted into a fort overlooking the harbor and the Monte containing 15 cannons. Other fortifications contained a similar number of arms that could overlook the waterways and the surrounding plains. The Dutch had little success in gaining any ground in Macau in the past, and they had even less of a chance in securing the colony now. Unfortunately for the Portuguese, this was not the case for their other colonies in the East Indies. In 1641 the Dutch managed to capture Malacca from the Portuguese, thereby successfully crippling the trade route of the Portuguese in the East.

Another blow to Portuguese trade took place in 1635 when Japan issued the *Sakoku* (closed door) Edict, which secluded it from trade with all foreigners. Japanese vessels were prohibited from traveling to foreign territories and the Japanese people were not allowed to emigrate. The Portuguese living in Japan were exiled to Macau, and the people of Japan were no longer allowed to purchase anything from the foreigners.

The senate of Macau attempted to create a peace in 1640 between the two cultures and dispatched messengers bearing 400 thousand taels to Japan. The ambassadors were seized by a shōgun and put to death, allegedly for not renouncing their faith, despite their neutral standing as ambassadors. The crew of the ship was allowed to return with a message from the Japanese emperor that should the king of Portugal or even the God of the Christians venture to land in Japan, the same death penalty would apply (Jesus 1902: 88).

A 1655 depiction of Macau

The wave of anti-Christianity came from the third shōgun Tokugawa Iemitsu who ruled from 1623-1651. Since 1545, beginning with the Portuguese, Japan had seen the arrival of numerous Europeans beginning the *Nanban* (southern barbarian) trade period. The actions of these European powers in the East Indies began to cause concern among the authorities in Japan. The Portuguese had conquered Malacca, while the Spanish had taken over the Philippines, all the while spreading Christianity to the lands they came in contact with. With the Sakoku Edict of 1635 Iemitsu hoped to halt the spread of Christianity. The edict offered rewards to the Japanese people who could offer any information on people who were secretly practicing Christianity or attempting to spread the religion during this period. The only foreign empire that was allowed to do business with the Japanese during this period and for the next 200 years was the Dutch East India Company, which was restricted to an isolated island.

At the same time in Europe, revolts began, led by John IV of Portugal. King Philip IV of Spain had increased the amount of taxes that the Portuguese merchants would have to pay on imports. Furthermore, he pushed efforts to make Portugal a providence of Spain rather than a kingdom in union with Spain. These measures led to a rebellion that the Spanish were ill-equipped to deal with due to the number of wars being fought at the time. As a result, John IV of Portugal was able to successfully take the throne from Philip IV of Spain. This, in turn led to the conflict later known as the Portuguese Restoration War until 1668 when Portugal could claim independence.

This break for independence from Spain in Europe resulted in a Spanish-Portuguese conflict in the East Indies. The governor of Manila, Don Sebastian de Corcuera, attempted to take control of Macau through forming allegiances with those in charge of Macau's commercial affairs. Corcuera then used this alliance to attempt to force the captain-general of Macau, Dom Sebastiao Lobo da Silveira to likewise make an alliance with the king of Spain and Manila. While Dom Sebastiao Lobo da Silveira favored such a deal, the senate protested, as did the people of Macau, which eventually led to a rebellion in the colony. Dom Sebastiao Lobo da Silveira was eventually seized and murdered by the mob before he could even be recalled to Goa for attempting to hand over the colony to the Spanish. In retaliation, the Spanish severed all ties with Macau, leaving the colony even more isolated.

During the 17th century, the Chinese empire and the Ming dynasty had been suffering a series of revolts, rebellions and outbreak of plagues. There were also economic setbacks that further crippled the empire. As much as the Chinese saw European goods as useless curiosities and trade as a privilege they let foreigners have, the empire depended on the flow of silver from these barbarian empires. Spain had discovered a new source of raw metals from South America which could easily be imported to China through Manila, but Philip IV of Spain needed the resources in Europe to pay for the numerous wars being fought. As such, efforts were put forth to ensure that the silver was not smuggled into China. The Sakoku Edict of 1635 also restricted the amount of silver able to be brought into China since the Europeans could no longer exchange European goods for silver. The lack of silver for merchants meant that taxes for the Ming dynasty could no longer be fully paid.

The disastrous state that the Ming dynasty was in led to a takeover by the Manchurian led Qing dynasty in 1644, but despite the sacking of Beijing and the death of the emperor, the Ming dynasty continued to reign in the southern Ming loyal regions, also known as the Southern Ming.

These loyal Ming forces were divided with multiple claimants to the throne and gradually they lost control of their respective territories. One of these claimants, Zheng Chenggong (or Ching Chi Kong), also known as Koxinga, led an anti-Qing force made up of a massive naval fleet in 1661. The naval fleet suffered massive amounts of damage following a hurricane, providing the Qing forces time to blockade rivers with iron chains and small gunboat rafts. It also allowed them time to strategize a counter-attack and Koxinga forces were ambushed. This ambush forced the retreat of Koxinga and his forces, effectively destroying any ambitions he had of overthrowing the Qing. Instead, he turned his eye toward the Dutch controlled Taiwan and drove them from the land thereby establishing the Kingdom of Tungning.

In order to protect their borders from the fleet of Koxinga, the Qing court ordered in 1662 that the coastal population retreat inland. To inhabit the coast during this period would result in death. This edict was also meant to apply to the Portuguese colony, mandating that all structures, including the forts, should be razed so that they wouldn't fall into the hands of Koxinga. The senate and the governor opted to try and pay for immunity to such measures, albeit unsuccessfully.

As a result, the Chinese lord of Heang-shan decided to take full advantage of the situation and extort as much money as possible from the people of Macau in order to allow them to remain on the coast. The Portuguese could either pay these fees, relocate to the interior, or starve. It was only due to the mediation of a Jesuit named Schall, who was present at the court in Peking, that the colony had a chance to remain. The Portuguese could pay a hefty fee in order to stay, but the imperial court nevertheless decided they needed to move to a new location down the Guangzhou River. This decree was disregarded and Macau was besieged by a Chinese fleet with any ships attempting to depart being burnt.

In 1667, the senate expressed the situation to the viceroy of India, which in turn attempted to establish an embassy at Peking with lavish gifts. In the meantime, trade had completely ceased in Macau, forcing the English to trade with the Dutch until Koxinga removed them from Taiwan. As a result, the English pushed for their own trading place in Guangzhou, but to the relief of the Portuguese, the English were forced to deal through Macau and the Portuguese were given exclusive trade rights in the area for an annual fee. Further relief was provided by the Kingdom of Siam, which sent a shipment of silver to the colony based on the good relations the two cultures had shared.

The British

The monopoly over trade would not last long, because in 1685, China became open to all foreign commerce. It was during this time that the British began dealing with the Yánghuò Háng (Ocean Trading House) in Guangzhou.

Near the end of the 17th century, the English were on uneasy terms with the Chinese but still trading regularly in Guangzhou. During this time, there was no establishment of rules or regulations regarding trade between Chinese merchants and the East India Company, which had been given a monopoly over trading in the region by the British Government. Moreover, there were no clear rules regarding daily life between the foreigners and the Chinese. At times, the British would obey certain Chinese laws, while other Chinese laws were ignored in favor of British laws. The East India Company tried to add stability to the region by empowering representatives with consular authority, but the Chinese never acknowledged this power. In the eyes of the Chinese, the foreigners were regarded as "barbarians" and were in need of a higher civilization, such as the Chinese. As a result, life in Guangzhou was relatively lawless, with merchants and sailors doing as they pleased. The threat of the Chinese ceasing trade with the merchants due to the British breaking Chinese laws was always a possibility, but the reality of the situation was that the Chinese merchants and administration was becoming increasingly wealthy through trades, tariffs and bribes.

The English merchants gradually began to settle in Guangzhou, or Canton as it was known to them, taking on wives from the local Chinese population and setting up establishments to teach English. Trade began growing between the two empires, and the first English man-of-war ship would arrive in the waters of China in 1742.

The establishment of the British in Guangzhou would take away a majority of the trade that had flowed through Macau. The British Empire at this time was vastly greater than that of the Portuguese, and it had the finances and naval fleets to support more aggressive tactics. The Portuguese, therefore, resorted to more subtle tactics to deal with the British trade competition. Using the xenophobic tendencies of the Chinese court to their advantage, the Portuguese would frequently offer negative anecdotes regarding the British motives resulting in complications for them (Brinkley 1904: 192).

Trade for the colony eventually improved, especially following the peace treaty between Spain and Portugal in 1668, which allowed trade between Manila and Macau. The Portuguese government, however, began imposing a number of restrictions on the colony and its trade. Portugal had also become dependent on England for protection with the Treaty of Methuen in 1703 due to the War of the Spanish Succession. This treaty reduced the taxes imposed on port wines imported into England while allowing England exclusive privileges for English trade goods in Portugal. The results were largely disastrous for Portugal. With the benefit of trade being shifted to the production of port wine, Portugal was only able to provide a rather limited export to England, whereas England was able to import vast quantities of more versatile goods such as cloth (which had a higher demand than port). As a result of having larger imports than exports, Portugal soon found itself indebted to England. The deficit was put off for a short time following the discovery of gold in the Portuguese colonies in Brazil, but the flow of colonial gold was neither large enough nor fast enough to pay off the debt.

The resulting problems Portugal had also stunted trade in Macau. At this time tea was becoming increasingly popular in England and Macau was offered a chance to benefit from this trade. The Chinese lords had grown frustrated with the English traders of Guangzhou and wished to shift the trade market from Guangzhou to Macau. This would have been extremely beneficial for the colony, but the acting governor, who was also a bishop, feared that the English religious practices would corrupt the Portuguese of Macau. As a result, trade was allowed to continue in Guangzhou and the Chinese court never made the colony another offer so generous.

In Guangzhou, the British and other foreign merchants had become increasingly skilled in avoiding certain taxes, bribing officials and getting around other prohibitive measures that could be found in Macau. By the end of the 18th century, trade had been reduced in Macau to approximately 8-10 ships that sailed mainly between the colony and Siam, while, despite all the tensions, trade carried on between the British and Chinese.

By the 19th century, Chinese tea, silks and porcelain were still in high demand in Britain, while there remained no demand from the Chinese for British products. For much of the 18th century, the East India Company was forced to ship boatloads of silver to China rather than manufactured goods, resulting in a deficit in trade and a strain on the economy. Britain's East India Company, which had its own naval and military force, was also in debt from wars being fought to control trade in India. To stop this debt from increasing, the East India Company, which still had a monopoly on trade in the region, began smuggling opium into Guangzhou (opium had been illegal in China since 1729). By 1793, the East India Company had created a monopoly on the purchase of opium in Bengal, India, thereby cutting out the Bengali merchants from the trade. The opium produced in Bengal was then sold in Calcutta (since it could not be sold in China) under the condition that it be sent to China. The East India Company would not carry the drug on their own ships and instead used private vessels so that they could deny any wrongdoing if the situation called for it. Smugglers then brought the opium to Lintin Island near Guangzhou, where it was sold. Profits from the opium were then used to purchase Chinese goods. It is estimated that around 900 tons of opium were being smuggled into China annually. Although the drug was already illegal in China, the Jiaqing Emperor (who reigned from 1796 to 1820) declared in 1799 that the import of opium was illegal. This did little to deter the buying and selling of the drug. In the early 19th century, large amounts of silver were being shipped from Guangzhou to India, resulting in a drain on the Chinese economy. In exchange for the illegal drug, the British demanded silver, which in turn was used to purchase tea and other Chinese goods. By 1838, the East India Company no longer had to send any silver laden ships - it could rely entirely on the selling of opium to purchase tea.

In 1808, a garrison of British troops were established in Macau in order to prevent attacks from French pirates due to an incident that took place in 1799 between the Royal Navy and a squadron of French and Spanish warships (as part of the French Revolutionary Wars between 1792 and 1802). The connection between the Portuguese in Macau and the British would be tested as the

British began smuggling more massive amounts of opium into Guangzhou, an act that was prohibited by the Chinese. Although the Portuguese were the first to start bringing the drug into the country, they had done so in amounts insignificant enough to have the drug be recognized for medicinal use. Meanwhile, the British had essentially been forced to smuggle the drug into China in order to pay for the high demand of tea from England. Since the Chinese demanded payment in silver and desired no other goods from England, the opium was being smuggled in and traded for silver or used to bribe officials, which the silver was then in turn used to purchase tea. Up until 1834, the East India Company had a monopoly on trade in the region and had done its best to maintain order while conducting their illegal operations in the region. However, after their charter ended in 1834, merchants were free to do as they pleased, resulting in a surge of opium through Guangzhou (Roberts 1999).

The smuggling of opium resulted in high tensions between the Chinese court and the British, culminating in the First Opium War. During this conflict, the relationship between the Portuguese and the British would be tested. As British ships clashed with the Chinese at the Battle of Chuenpi in 1839, the British maneuvered to Macau and sought a safe haven. The British superintendent, Captain Charles Elliot, requested of Governor Adrião Acácio da Silveira Pinto permission on March 22, 1839 to allow the British vessels to unload goods in the Macau port (Jesus 1902: 255). Pinto, however, was aware that to do so would risk angering the Chinese lords, who, as they had done multiple times in the past, could swiftly cut off provisions and starve the Portuguese. Furthermore, even though the British had already been refused by the Portuguese, the Chinese emperor, Daoguang, issued a decree in 1840 that all material assistance to the British was to cease.

Of course, the British were equipped to handle the Chinese in this conflict, and in August 1840 the British returned to Macau with land forces. The British marines were able to quickly defeat the Chinese soldiers that controlled the land bridge separating Macau from the rest of mainland China, thereby liberating Macau from the constant threat of starvation. Now the Portuguese were willing to be pro-British in the conflict between the two empires and allowed the British ships to dock at Macau. This strategic alliance allowed the British to have a valuable port in southern China as a base of operations to begin their campaign down the Pearl River and toward Guangzhou. The British would be successful in their battle against the Chinese, with the First Opium War ending in 1842 and resulting in the leasing of Hong Kong to the British.

Autonomy

A 19th century panorama of Macau

The result of British control over Hong Kong was that there were even fewer trade opportunities for the Portuguese. The Treaty of Peking, which had ended the war and forced China to lease Hong Kong to the British, had shown to the Portuguese that the Chinese court could be taken advantage of, so the Portuguese at first refused to pay more rent to Chinese officials in order to proclaim Macau as independent. This attempt, however, was not met well by the Chinese and rent was deemed necessary, thereby keeping the Portuguese in a derogatory position. The attitude for the independence of Macau at this time was still strong in the colony, while the Chinese did not recognize the colony as anything more than their land occupied by foreigners who were still at the mercy of the surrounding Chinese lords.

With the Chinese unwilling to acknowledge Macau's independence and the British unwilling to assist the Portuguese colony in its struggle for recognition, the colony struggled to maintain its commercial interests against Hong Kong. In an attempt to generate income, the colony declared gambling legal in 1844, resulting in Macau becoming a hub of illegal activities (Cremer 1987).

Eventually, the Portuguese made the bold decision to abolish the Chinese custom house of Macau, the main source of income for the colony, and issued a royal decree on November 20, 1845 declaring Macau a free port. The appointed governor at the time, Captain Ferreira do Amaral, was granted permission to assert the absolute autonomy of the colony. Unfortunately for the colony, the timing of this declaration came at the same time a civil war broke out in Portugal, resulting in resources being tied up and no reinforcements being dispatched for the colony. Thus, three years after the proclamation of independence and the abolishment of the custom house, there still stood a Chinese custom house in Macau, and the enforcement of the freedom of the port was left to artillery. Given the confused status of the colony, trade during this period became stagnate, and the Chinese lords used the existence of the custom house as a means to taunt Amaral over the status of the colony. While Amaral demanded the closure of the custom house, the Chinese lords insisted that the custom house needed to remain as a means to protect their trade interests against smuggling.

Amaral

Amaral was undeterred and insisted Macau was a free port. He formally removed the final custom house on March 5, 1849. Additionally, whenever the Chinese lords were to visit Macau in the future, they would be treated as and accorded the honors due to foreign representatives. Amaral went on to disband the senate and do away with the Chinese laws that were displayed at the senate house in a show of Macau's independence from Chinese rule (Jesus 1902: 281).

In August 1849, Amaral was brutally assassinated by a group of Chinese men, leaving control of the colony in chaos with no senate and no governor. Seemingly anticipating this scenario, Chinese troops began assembling in the nearby vicinity of Macau. The Chinese were intent on reclaiming Macau as a Chinese territory and sent more than 2,000 soldiers against the 120 Portuguese based in Macau. The Chinese soldiers were sent from Pak-sa-leang, a nearby Chinese fort, but an offensive against this fort was led by Vicente Nicolao de Mesquita, along with 36 men and a howitzer cannon, and against all odds, the Portuguese men led by Mesquita were able to successfully take the fort and raise the Portuguese flag there.

A depiction of Amaral's assassination

The local Chinese lord in charge of the fort was executed, prompting the Portuguese to request assistance from the British in fear of retaliation. British marines led by Captain Troubridge arrived at Macau and strengthened the defenses of the colony against surprise attacks while also leaving a man-of-war ship in the port. The French and Spanish followed the British example and sent reinforcements as well. The Portuguese did away with the barrier wall that the Chinese had constructed to keep the foreigners isolated, and in its place outposts and forts were established.

Foreign governments acknowledged the independence of Macau, and the relationship between China and Portugal continued with Macau acting as a neutral port for the Chinese in periods of conflict, such as the Taiping Rebellion that was taking place during this time. During this rebellion, the Chinese believed that if they acknowledged Macau as a neutral territory in the conflict, then it would not be a contested land during the conflict. This proved to be the case to the satisfaction of the Qing court. Still, the Portuguese of Macau desired to have in writing that their colony was independent of the Chinese court. On August 13, 1862, a treaty was drawn up at Tientsin which, among various other trade articles, would recognize Macau as an integral Portuguese colony. When the treaty was to be ratified on June 17, 1864, the Chinese representatives of the court did not appear in Tientsin. The current governor of Macau, José Rodrigues Coelho do Amaral, demanded to know why there was no Qing court representation, and he received the response that certain points in the treaty needed to be rewritten or addressed. Such communications carried on between the two empires for the next two decades, with neither side being satisfied. In the same vein, the Chinese court frequently made excuses as to why the treaty could not be ratified.

Circumstances changed as the Chinese continued to struggle with the opium imported by the British. It was by now recognized that the Chinese authorities could not stop the flow of opium, and so the Qing court attempted to gain more control over the drug in order to collect revenue from its import. To do so, the Chinese court required the cooperation of Macau, resulting in Chinese representatives establishing contact with the Portuguese court in Lisbon in 1887. In return for the independence of Macau, the colony was to cooperate with the Chinese regarding opium in the same manner that was being undertaken in Hong Kong. On December 1, 1887 the Treaty of Peking was ratified, thereby officially recognizing the colony 330 years after the Portuguese had first established its questionable status.

The status of Macau would come into question again and be adjusted in 1951, when the colony became recognized as an Overseas Province with closer integration with Portugal. No longer would Macau have the autonomy that it had been granted in the past, largely in part due to the developments in technology that allowed easier lines of communication and travel that had been developed. Macau would now have elected representation at the National Assembly in Lisbon, but the finances of the Province would still largely remain under the control of a governor appointed in Lisbon (Ride and Ride 1999: 54-56).

In 1987, Macau and the government of the People's Republic of China reached an agreement for Macau to officially be returned to China in 1999. Given that Macau had been established based on free trade and capitalism, China, now a socialist country, agreed that Macau would be allowed to retain a significant amount of autonomy as far as economic practices were concerned until 2049.

Following the handover of Portuguese Macau to China, the legalization of gambling that had been passed in 1844 to counter the trade revenue lost to the British in Hong Kong transformed Macau into the "Las Vegas of Asia" in the 21st century.

Online Resources

Other books about Chinese history by Charles River Editors

Bibliography

Arnold, David. 2002. *The Age of Discovery, 1400-1600*. London: Routledge

Boxer, Charles Ralph. 1948. *Fidalgos in the Far East 1550-1770*. Oxford: Oxford University Press

Brinkley, Captain F. 1904. *China: Its History Arts and Literature vol. X.* London: T.C. & E.C. Jack

Chengzhi, Xie; Chunxiang, Li; Yinqiu, Cui; Dawei, Cai; Haijing, Wang; Hong, Zhu; and Hui, Zhou. 2007. Mitochondrial DNA analysis of ancient Sampula population in Xinjiang. In: *Progress in Natural Science*, vol. 17, pp 927–33

Chinese Repository. Vol. I.: From May 1832 to April 1835. 1832. Canton: Printed for the Proprietors

Christopoulos, Lucas. 2012. Hellenes and Romans in Ancient China. *Sino-Platonic Papers*, 230. *http://www.sino-platonic.org/complete/spp230_hellenes_romans_in_china.pdf* Accessed: 20 April 2018

Cremer, R.D. 1987. *Macau: City of Commerce and Culture.* China SAR: Macau

Holt, Frank L. 1989. *Alexander the Great and Bactria: The Formation of a Greek Frontier in Central Asia.* New York: E.J. Brill

Hunt, Patrick. 2007. *Byzantine Silk: Smuggling and Espionage in the 6th Century CE.* *http://altmarius.ning.com/profiles/blogs/byzantine-silk-smuggling-and-espionage-in-the-6th-century-ce* Accessed: 22 April 2018.

Jesus, Carlos Augusto Montalto. 1902. *Historic Macau.* Hong Kong: Kelly & Walsh

Parker, Edward H. (trans.) 1890. *China's Intercourse with Europe.* Shanghai: Kelly and Walsh

Pliny the Elder. *The Natural History.* Bostock, John and Riley, Henry Thomas (trans.) 1855.

Rémusat, Abel. 1829. *Nouveaux mélanges asiatiques.* Paris: Schubart et Heideloff

Ride, Lindsay and Ride, May. 1999. *The Voices of Macau Stones.* Hong Kong: Hong Kong University Press

Roberts, J.A.G. 1999. *A Concise History of China.* Cambridge: Harvard University Press

Silberman, Neil Asher (Editor in Chief). 2012. *The Oxford Companion to Archaeology (Second Edition).* Oxford: Oxford university Press

Southey, Robert (ed). 1812. *Omniana or Horæ Otiosiores.* London: Longman, Hurst, Rees, Orme, and Brown

Tarn, W.W. 1966. *The Greeks in Bactria and India.* London: Cambridge University Press

Tsai, Shih-Shan Henry. 2001. *Perpetual Happiness: The Ming Emperor Yongle*. Washington: University of Washington Press

Young, Gary K. 2001. *Rome's Eastern Trade: International Commerce and Imperial Policy 31 BCE - CE 305*. London: Routledge

Free Books by Charles River Editors

We have brand new titles available for free most days of the week. To see which of our titles are currently free, click on this link.

Discounted Books by Charles River Editors

We have titles at a discount price of just 99 cents everyday. To see which of our titles are currently 99 cents, click on this link.